Racing cars
and cycles

Peter Firmin

A & C Black · London

Contents

With grateful thanks to the following people who helped to make the
models for this book: Dorian, Lewis, Ruth, Olivia, Sam, Laurence and Oliver.

A CIP catalogue record for this book is available from the British Library.

First published 1994 by A & C Black (Publishers) Limited
35 Bedford Row, London WC1R 4JH

ISBN 0-7136-3624-6

Filmset by Rowland Phototypesetting Limited
Bury St Edmunds, Suffolk.
Printed in Great Britain by
Cambus Litho Limited, East Kilbride.

About this book

In this book, there are detailed instructions to help you make racing cars, trucks, tractors and many other working models. It begins by showing you how to make simple "pushalong" models with free-turning wheels. Making these will help you to tackle the more complicated models such as the fire-engine, tractor and tricycle. They use elastic bands and spring wire to drive them along and will take time to make – so don't try to do everything in one go.

On page 5 there's a list of things you will need. It's a good idea to have two large boxes to put everything in – one for all your materials and one for your tools. Most of the materials you will need are things you can find around the house; things which would normally be thrown away. Large boxes and cardboard tubes are often thrown away by shops. The larger your selection of boxes, the more varied and interesting your models will be, so start collecting.

You will need to buy some materials, such as PVA glue and wire. But you can save money by sharing these and your tools with friends.

I hope you'll have fun racing these models. But remember – speed isn't everything. You can also award points for the longest distance travelled, the best movement, the most original model or the funniest legs.

Glossary

This glossary explains some of the words used in the book and describes the various parts used to make the models. All words in the glossary appear in the text in **bold** type.

Adjacent   next to.

Axle   a length of wire which connects a pair of wheels.

axle

Strong coathanger wire makes a good axle.

Bearing   a hole or tube in which the **axle** turns.

straw bearing

The sides of this vehicle act as bearings.

Crank   a right-angled bend in a wire **axle** which turns circular movement into backwards and forwards (**reciprocal**) movement.

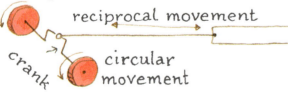

reciprocal movement

circular movement

crank

Diagonally   slantwise.
Driveband   a band that passes on movement from one part of a machine to another.

elastic

elastic band

string

Energy   the power of doing work.

Gravity   the pull of an object towards the Earth.

It wasn't my fault - it was gravity.

Hub   the central part of a wheel which turns, or rotates, on or with the **axle**.

hub

A 2 cm slice of cork makes a good hub.

Potential energy   stored **energy** waiting to do work.

Pulley   a free running drum or wheel which allows the **driveband** to turn easily over an **axle**.

A cotton reel makes a good pulley.

Reciprocal movement   moving backwards and forwards.

Rotary movement   moving round and round.

Washer   a bead placed between two moving parts which reduces **friction**.

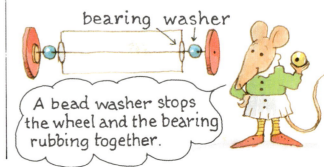

bearing washer

A bead washer stops the wheel and the bearing rubbing together.

Tools, equipment . . .

awl for making holes
block of wood
brushes
bulldog clips and pegs
coloured paints
craft knife
hacksaw
hammer
hand drill

masking tape
nails
newspaper to work on
paperclips
pencil and ruler
pens
pins
pliers
PVA glue

school glue
scissors
sponge for putting on paint
staple gun
stapler
sticky tape
vice
white emulsion paint
wire cutters
wood glue

and materials

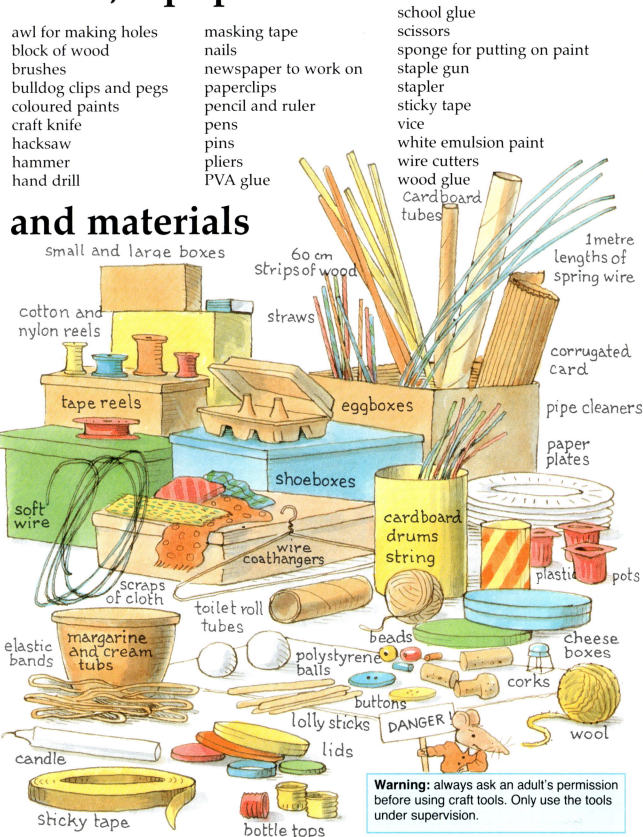

cardboard tubes

small and large boxes

60 cm strips of wood

1 metre lengths of spring wire

cotton and nylon reels

straws

corrugated card

tape reels

eggboxes

pipe cleaners

paper plates

soft wire

shoeboxes

cardboard drums string

plastic pots

wire coathangers

scraps of cloth

toilet roll tubes

beads

cheese boxes

elastic bands

margarine and cream tubs

polystyrene balls

corks

buttons

lolly sticks

DANGER !

wool

candle

lids

sticky tape

bottle tops

Warning: always ask an adult's permission before using craft tools. Only use the tools under supervision.

5

Useful tips

Before you begin, read these pages carefully. They will tell you which tools to use for which jobs, and how to use them safely.

Cutting

Where possible, use scissors to cut card and boxes. The best sort of scissors have rounded ends. Never point scissors at anyone.

If you want to use a craft knife, ask an adult. Make sure the knife is sharp. Protect your work surface by cutting on to a thick pad of newspaper on top of a piece of card.

Pricking

If you are using an awl to prick holes in a box, or cutting a box with a knife, put a block of wood inside the box so you've got a hard surface to press down on.

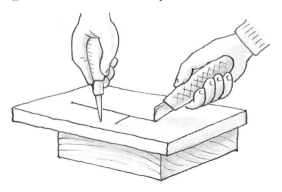

Gluing

Use small pegs or bulldog clips to hold glued pieces of card together. Then you can get on with something else while the glue is drying.

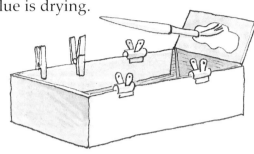

To join boxes, glue the surfaces together and tape the joins with masking tape. The models can be made stronger and are easier to paint if you paste paper over all the surfaces first.

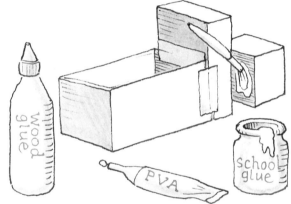

Joining elastic bands

Join elastic bands together like this:

Join them to string like this:

Join them to an **axle** like this:

Cutting wire

Cut thin wire with pliers.

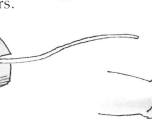

Thick wire and wooden dowel should be held securely in a vice and cut with a hacksaw. Keep your fingers clear of the saw.

Hammering

Before hammering nails into hardwood, drill a fine hole with a hand drill. This will stop the wood splitting.

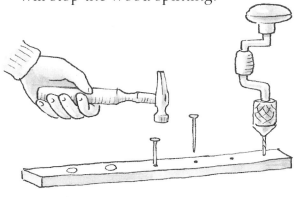

Always hammer on to a block of wood in case the nails come through the other side.

If the nails do come through, make them safe by tapping the points over.

Linking wire

Soft wire can be linked to a **crank** with a coil. Use pliers to grasp the first turn of the coil, and then twist the wire round the **crank** with your fingers.

The wire should be loose enough to allow the coil to turn on the **crank**. If not, work it round until it loosens.

Stapling

A staple gun is useful for fixing lids to corks to make wheels. Always aim the gun straight down on to a surface.

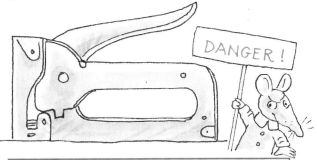

DANGER!

Warning: if you use a staple gun make sure an adult is present.

Making wheels

Wheels are the most important part of these models. Once you have learnt to make a selection of different wheels, it's easy to make any models you may invent yourself.

Each set of wheels has the following:

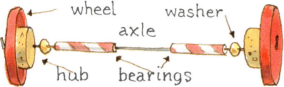

For a very simple racer, put wheels on to an empty square plastic bottle.

> To make a pair of wheels you will need: 2 identical jam jar lids, 2 pieces of cork about 2cm long, a straight piece of coathanger wire about 8cm longer than the width of the bottle, 2 beads, 2 pieces of straw about 3cm long and some nails.

1 Make holes through the centre of the jam jar lids and the corks with an awl.

Always use a block underneath.

2 Nail each jam jar lid to a cork, making sure you match up the holes. The cork acts as a **hub**.

3 The coathanger wire is the **axle**. Thread a wheel and a bead on to the wire. Then thread on the two straw **bearings**, the other bead and the other wheel. The beads act as **washers**.

4 Hold the **axle** in a vice and bend up the ends of the wire to secure the wheels as shown.

5 Make a second set of wheels in the same way. Attach the wheels to a plastic bottle by taping the straw **bearings** to the base of the bottle.

6 Cut a small hole in the top of the bottle for the seat.

These wheels are called running wheels. They do not need to grip the **axle**, but turn freely on it or in the **bearings**.

Free wheel racing

Once you've made the wheels for the plastic bottle racer, it's easy to adapt them to suit other models. Here are some ideas you can try.

This early racing car is made from a rectangular cracker box.

You will need: a rectangular cracker box, 2 sets of wheels (see page 8), made out of the thin metal lids from baby food jars.

1 Cut along the thick black lines and fold along the dotted lines.

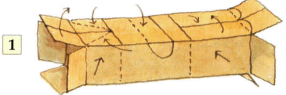

2 Following the directions of the arrows, fold in the ends of the box and glue the flaps together.

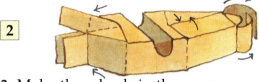

3 Make the wheels in the same way as the wheels for the plastic bottle racer on page 8. Attach the straw **bearings** to your racer with tape.

This truck has three sets of wheels.

You will need: 3 boxes (one for the open back about 18 × 10 × 12cm and two smaller ones for the cab and bonnet), 3 sets of wheels (see page 8), one pair made from plastic film can lids and two pairs made from metal bottle lids.

1 Cut and glue down the top side of the big box as shown.

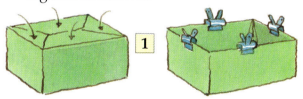

2 Glue the two smaller boxes together to make the cab and bonnet. Glue these to the big box.

3 Make the front wheels from film can lids. Use metal bottle lids for the two sets of back wheels. Attach the wheels to the truck by taping the straw **bearings** to the base of the truck.

A cork just fits a bottle lid.

The back wheels for this racing car are made and attached in a slightly different way to those on page 8.

You will need: a box about 18 × 9 × 5cm, card, 2 matchboxes, 2 sets of wheels (see page 8), (one pair made from plastic film can lids and one pair made from thin round cheese boxes).

1 Cut and fold the front of the box as shown. This will give the racing car its distinctive shape.

Cut along the black lines.

Fold along the dotted lines.

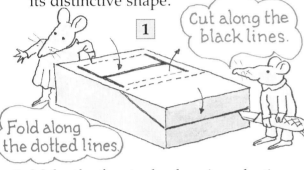

2 Make the front wheels using plastic film can lids and attach them to the model (see page 8).

3 The back wheels are made out of thin cheese spread boxes. Make a small hole through the centre of the boxes and the slices of cork.

4 Glue each box together with a piece of cork inside matching up the hole in the cork with the holes in the box. The cork acts as the **hub** of the wheel.

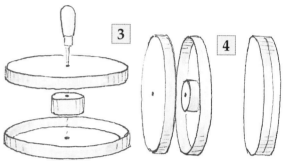

5 Make a small hole in each side of the box at A. Thread the wire **axle** through the holes. Slide a bead and a wheel on to each end of wire. Bend the ends of the wire to secure the wheels.

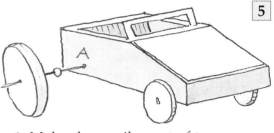

6 Make the spoiler out of two matchboxes and a strip of card.

Start the race on a slope or just give the cars a good push. The winner of the race could be the fastest car or the longest runner. You could also award points for the smartest looking car.

Ideas for how to decorate your models and how to make the drivers can be found on pages 30–32.

Twisted elastic power

The models on the next three pages use the power of twisted elastic to drive them along. A twisted elastic band has **potential energy** which is released as the band unwinds.

The cotton reel tank, one of the oldest moving toys, is powered by twisted elastic.

> You will need: a long cotton reel, a slice of candle 1cm thick, a matchstick, an elastic band and a lolly stick or strip of wood.

1 Use an awl to poke out the wick from the slice of candle.

2 Thread the elastic band through the cotton reel and secure it at one end with a matchstick.

3 Thread the other end of the elastic band through the hole in the candle and secure it with the lolly stick or strip of wood. Wind up the stick and watch the tank go.

You can make a tank out of any drum. Always use a piece of candle or another type of **washer**, so that the stick clears the edges of the drum and turns smoothly.

Decorate the stick with a paper figure to make the race more fun.

A drum roll

The cotton reel tank is pushed along by an arm, the stick, which touches the ground. If you use a large drum, with a short heavy arm which does not touch the ground, the drum will move along using the force of **gravity**.

You will need: 2 identical margarine tubs with lids, a small cotton reel, a slice of candle 1cm thick with the wick removed (see page 11), a matchstick, a large elastic band, a piece of wire 12cm long bent at one end to make a hook and a piece of Plasticine weighing about 20–30g.

1 Cut a hole, 1cm in diameter, in the centre of each lid and the bottom of each tub.

1

2 Put a lid on to each tub. Join the bottoms of the tubs together with sticky tape to make a drum.

2

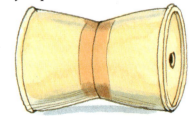

3 Thread the elastic band through the drum and secure it at one end with the matchstick and some sticky tape.

Use a bent wire to pull it through.

3

4 Thread the other end through the cotton reel and the slice of candle. Secure the end with the wire hook.

4

5 Wind up the hook, add the Plasticine weight and let go.

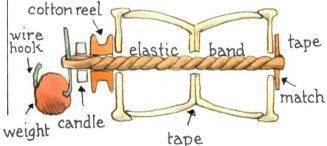

cotton reel
wire hook
elastic band
tape
match
weight candle
tape

As the elastic band unwinds, the wire hook moves upwards, but the weight of the Plasticine pulls the hook back down. This movement makes the drum roll move along.

5

You can use heavy metal washers or nuts for the weight.

The drum road-roller

You will need: 2 identical 1 kilo putty tubs with lids, 2 large elastic bands, 2 beads, 30cm of strong coathanger wire, a small drum, eg. a spice pot, 2 boxes for the cab and body and a set of running wheels (see page 8), made from jam jar lids.

1 Join the bottoms of the tubs together with sticky tape.

2 Take off the lids and make a hole with a diameter of 1cm in the centre of each.

3 Make two holes in the bottom of each tub with an awl. The holes should be about 2cm apart. Put on the lids.

4 Thread two elastic bands through the pots – make sure that the bands go through different holes in the bottoms of the tubs. Thread a bead on to the bands at each end to act as **washers**.

5 Make a fork from the coathanger wire as shown. It needs to be about 3cm wider than your drum. Thread it through the elastic bands on each side of the drum.

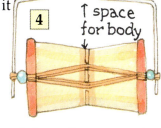

↑ space for body

6 Make the body of the roller using the small drum and the boxes. Attach the running wheels under the cab.

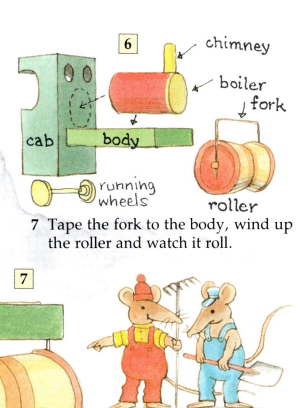

chimney

boiler

fork

cab body

running wheels

roller

7 Tape the fork to the body, wind up the roller and watch it roll.

Stretched elastic power

There is **potential energy** in a stretched elastic band. The **energy** is released as the elastic pulls back to its original size.

The models on the next few pages are powered by stretched elastic bands.

They have a set of running wheels (see page 8), at the front and a set of driving wheels at the back which drive the models along. Driving wheels are made in the same way as running wheels but are fitted in a different way:

a the driving wheel **axle** must run through the model rather than underneath it;

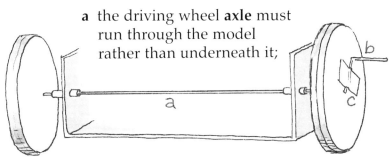

b the driving wheel **axle** has a handle. Leave an extra bit of wire at one end to make this;

c driving wheels need to grip the **axle**. Use sticky tape to tape each end of the **axle** to a wheel.

A quick ride

You will need: a strong shoebox, an elastic band, a paperclip, 3 pieces of drinking straw (one about 8cm long and two about 3cm long), a set of running wheels (see page 8), made from jam jar lids and a set of driving wheels (see above), made from thin cheese spread boxes.

1 Make the running wheels and attach them to the box.

2 Make a hole in each side of the box at A and glue a 3cm piece of straw into each hole as a **bearing**.

3 Thread the driving **axle** through the **bearings** and attach the driving wheels. Leave enough wire at one end to make a handle.

4 Join one end of the elastic **driveband** to the **axle** at B. Make a small hole at C. Thread the other end of the elastic band through the hole and secure it with a paperclip. Turn the handle on the **axle** to wind up the elastic.

> When you let the model go, the stretched elastic pulls back and unwinds from the axle, turning the wheels.

A longer ride

The more elastic there is to wind up, the further your model will travel.

You will need: the same materials as those for the quick ride (see page 14), plus a piece of wooden dowel 4cm longer than the width of the shoebox, a cotton reel and 4 or 5 elastic bands joined together to measure about 45cm.

1 Make and attach the running wheels and the driving wheels (see page 14).

2 Make a hole in each side of the box at A. Push the dowel through one of the holes and thread on the cotton reel which acts as a **pulley**. Push the dowel through the other hole.

3 Attach the elastic **driveband** to the driving wheel **axle** and take it round the **pulley**. Make a small hole at B and secure the end of the elastic with a paperclip.

Turn the handle to wind up the elastic

A faster ride

You will get a more powerful model if you use two **drivebands** at the same time.

You will need: the same materials as those for the longer ride (see page 14), plus one more cotton reel and one more set of elastic bands.

1 Make the model in the same way as the longer ride, but fit two cotton reel pulleys on to the wooden dowel.

2 Attach each set of elastic **drivebands** to the driving wheel **axle** and take each round a separate **pulley**. Secure the ends of the elastic bands as before.

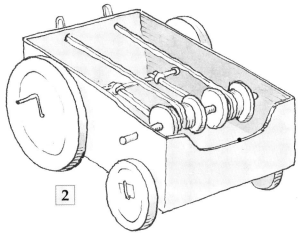

You may find the elastic bands become tangled on the **axle**. If so, replace half of the elastic with string, and attach the string-end to the **axle**. When the wheels are wound up, the string winds round the **axle**, stretching the elastic.

Can you invent a model which makes use of the extra length of string?

There are some ideas on the next few pages

15

The fire-engine

You will need: 3 boxes (1 strong corrugated card box, about 30 × 17 × 17cm, 2 smaller boxes, about 20 × 15 × 5cm and 11 × 9 × 5cm), wood for ladder (2 strips each 60cm long, 7 strips each 6cm long, 2 lengths of dowel about 8cm long), wood for ladder rack (2 strips each 6cm long, 1 strip 7cm long), 3 cotton reel pulleys, 2 pieces of straw about 3cm long, 20cm of dowel, 30 × 10cm of corrugated card, a paperclip, 80cm of string, 70cm of elastic bands, a set of running wheels (see page 8), made from jam jar lids and a set of driving (see page 14), wheels made from cheese spread boxes.

The power to drive the engine is provided by strong elastic bands joined together to make a length of 70cm. These are joined to an 80cm length of string.

1 Fold in and glue the flaps on one side of the big box to give it extra strength. This is the underside.

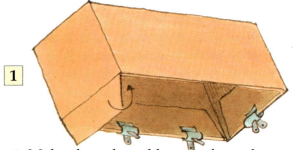

2 Make the cab and bonnet from the other two boxes and glue and tape them to the big box. Leave to dry.

3 Make the front running wheels and attach them to the bonnet.

4 Cut holes in the top and back of the large box at A. Make the ladder rack by gluing the wood together. Make holes at B and fit the rack to the fire-engine.

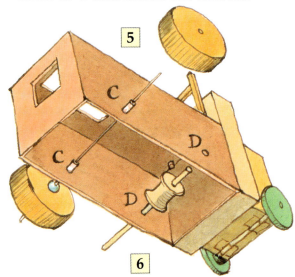

ladder rack

5 Make holes in the sides at C. Glue a 3cm piece of straw into each hole to act as a **bearing**. Make the driving wheels from the cheese boxes. To give the driving wheels extra grip, wrap them with corrugated card. Thread the driving **axle** through the holes at C and attach the wheels.

6 Make holes in both sides of the body at D. Thread the 20cm length of dowel through the holes fitting a cotton reel **pulley** as you go.

7 Make the ladder leaving a 7cm space between each rung. The seven middle rungs can be nailed or taped to the sides. The end rungs are made of dowel. Make holes with a hand drill and thread the dowel through, fitting the **pulleys** as you go.

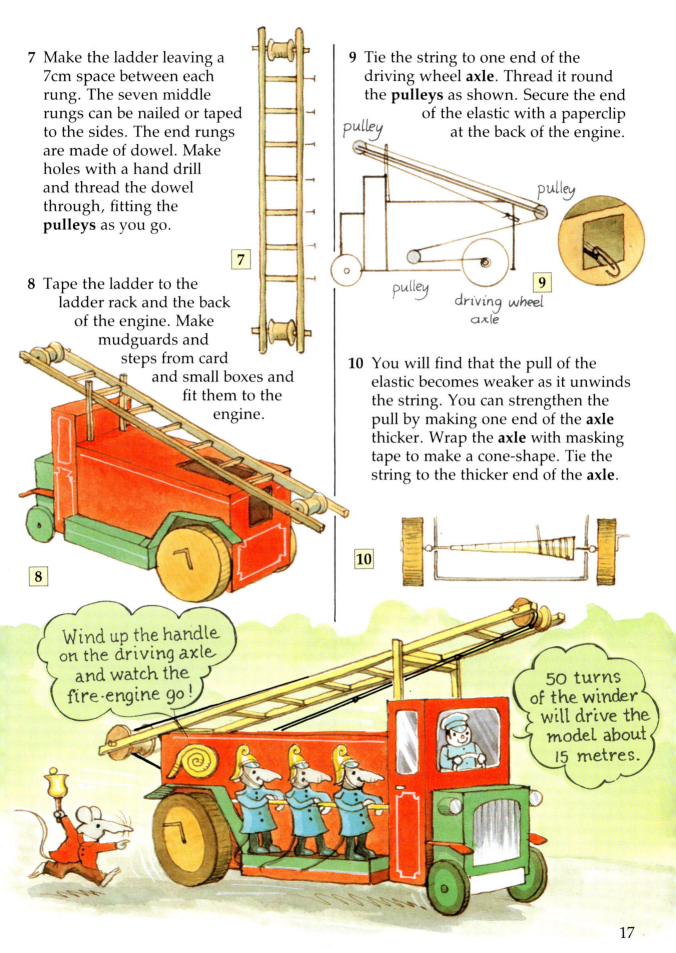

8 Tape the ladder to the ladder rack and the back of the engine. Make mudguards and steps from card and small boxes and fit them to the engine.

9 Tie the string to one end of the driving wheel **axle**. Thread it round the **pulleys** as shown. Secure the end of the elastic with a paperclip at the back of the engine.

pulley

pulley

pulley

driving wheel axle

10 You will find that the pull of the elastic becomes weaker as it unwinds the string. You can strengthen the pull by making one end of the **axle** thicker. Wrap the **axle** with masking tape to make a cone-shape. Tie the string to the thicker end of the **axle**.

Wind up the handle on the driving axle and watch the fire-engine go!

50 turns of the winder will drive the model about 15 metres.

The tractor

The power to drive the tractor is provided by 50cm of elastic bands joined to 50cm of thin string.

You will need: 5 boxes (1 strong cereal box, about 24 × 12 × 4cm, 4 smaller boxes for the engine and seat), 2 strips of strong card 3.5 × 40cm, 9cm of dowel, a long cotton reel, 12 matchsticks or cocktail sticks, a straw, a pin or bulldog clip, thin card, 50cm of elastic bands, 50cm of thin string, a set of running wheels (see page 8), made out of small metal lids and a set of driving wheels (see page 14), made out of thick cheese boxes.

1 Fold in and glue the ends of the big box. Cut a large square hole in the bottom.

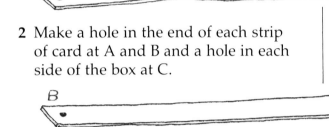

2 Make a hole in the end of each strip of card at A and B and a hole in each side of the box at C.

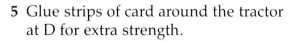

3 Glue the strips of card to the box, matching up the holes at A with those at C.

4 Make the hay turner. This is a long cotton reel with matchsticks or cocktail sticks glued around the ends. Thread the cotton reel on to the dowel and attach it to the tractor by inserting the ends of the dowel through the holes at B.

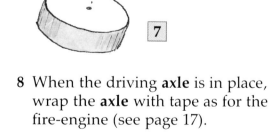

5 Glue strips of card around the tractor at D for extra strength.

6 Make the front running wheels and attach them to the base of the tractor with a straw **bearing**.

7 Thread the driving **axle** through the box at A and fit the driving wheels.

8 When the driving **axle** is in place, wrap the **axle** with tape as for the fire-engine (see page 17).

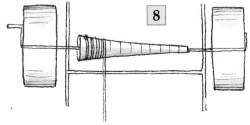

9 Tie the string to the thick end of the driving wheel **axle**. Take the string round the hay turner and back inside the tractor as shown.

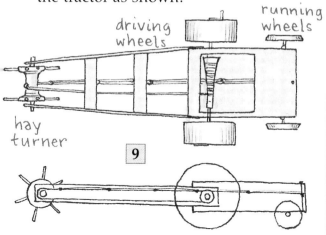

10 Secure the end of the elastic bands at the front of the tractor with a bulldog clip or pin.

11 Make the tractor body from the other boxes. The seat is half a small box cut in two **diagonally**.

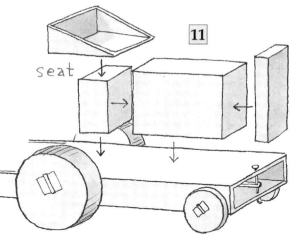

12 Make the tractor driver following the instructions on page 30.

30 turns of the winder will drive the tractor about 10 metres.

The hay turner will rotate as the string unwinds.

Spring wire power

There is **potential energy** in a piece of bent spring wire. The **energy** is released as the wire straightens.

The wire must be very springy. The best kind of wire is 16 gauge piano wire which you can buy in model shops. It usually comes in 1 metre lengths and because it isn't permanently fixed to the model it can be taken off and used to make other models.

These tricycles will travel about 18 metres on 45 turns of the winder.

The pedalling legs look very
funny and you can award extra
points for the funniest legs!

21

The tricycle

The power to drive the tricycle is provided by two 1 metre lengths of piano wire joined together at one end to a metre of thin string.

1 Cut box 1 in half. Make 1cm cuts up two **adjacent** corners on each box. Fold out the tabs.

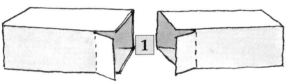

2 Glue these two half boxes to the end corners of box 2.

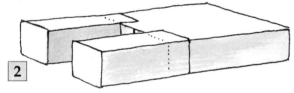

3 Glue boxes 3 and 4 together to make the seat and base of the handlebars. Fix them to the other boxes.

4 Tape a small strip of wood across the top of the handlebar base to make the handlebars. Tape a piece of straw across the top of the seat.

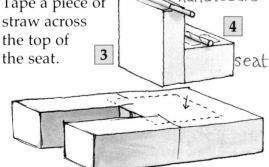

5 Fold in and glue the back end flaps of box 2 and strengthen the sides if necessary with thick card.

6 Make holes in each side of box 2 at A and holes in the centre of two film can lids. Tape the lids to the box at A, taking care to match up the holes. The lids will be strong **bearings** for the **axle**.

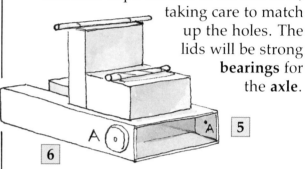

7 Make and fit the driving wheels and thicken the **axle** with tape (see page 17).

8 Fold up and glue the top of box 2 behind the seat so that you can see the driving **axle** from above.

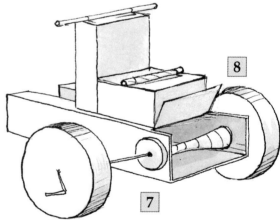

9 Make the tricycle wheel in the same way as the driving wheels. Thread the wheel on to a 20 cm wire **axle**. Slide a 3cm piece of straw and a bead on to each side of the wheel. Make two right-angled bends in both ends of the wire to make the pedals.

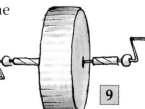

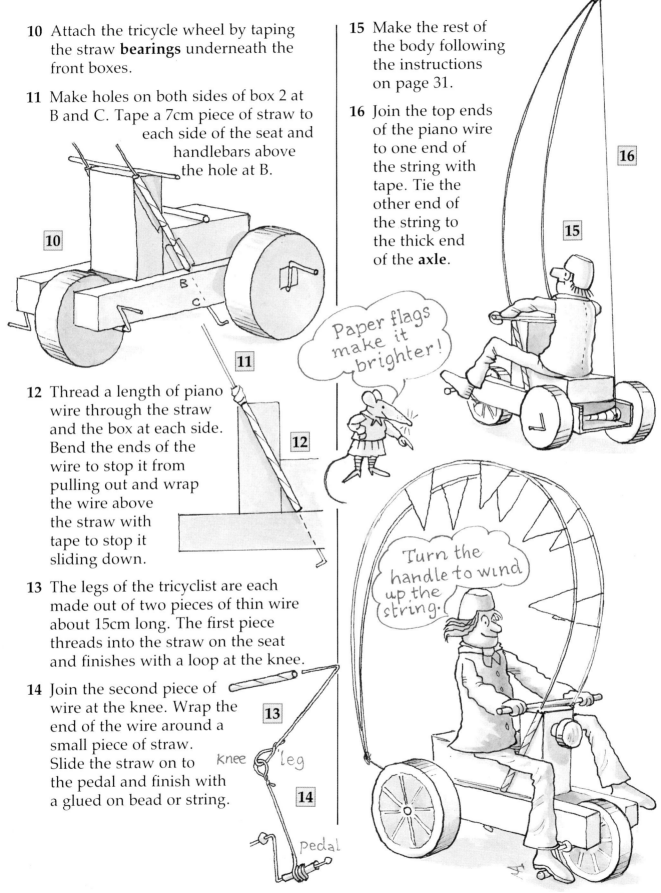

10 Attach the tricycle wheel by taping the straw **bearings** underneath the front boxes.

11 Make holes on both sides of box 2 at B and C. Tape a 7cm piece of straw to each side of the seat and handlebars above the hole at B.

12 Thread a length of piano wire through the straw and the box at each side. Bend the ends of the wire to stop it from pulling out and wrap the wire above the straw with tape to stop it sliding down.

13 The legs of the tricyclist are each made out of two pieces of thin wire about 15cm long. The first piece threads into the straw on the seat and finishes with a loop at the knee.

14 Join the second piece of wire at the knee. Wrap the end of the wire around a small piece of straw. Slide the straw on to the pedal and finish with a glued on bead or string.

knee   leg

pedal

15 Make the rest of the body following the instructions on page 31.

16 Join the top ends of the piano wire to one end of the string with tape. Tie the other end of the string to the thick end of the **axle**.

Paper flags make it brighter!

Turn the handle to wind up the string.

23

Cranks and linked movement

The horses pulling these carts and wagons are attached to a **crank** on the front **axle**. The **crank** turns **rotary movement** into **reciprocal movement**, so that the horses look as if they're galloping as the models race along.

Also, by carefully adjusting the length of the reins, you can make the driver's arms jerk up and down so that he seems to be shaking the reins.

It's important to make sure that the shafts, the bars between the horse and the wagon, are glued high enough off the ground so that the horse's legs clear the ground as the model moves along.

If you make the horse's legs from thick wool or pieces of straw, they will move as the horse moves.

You will find details showing how to make the covered wagon on the next two pages. You can also try making your own cart or carriage to fit the same base.

The covered wagon

You will need: 2 boxes (box 1 is a strong flat box about 30 × 16 × 3cm, box 2 is a short box e.g. a tissue box), 2 paper plates, 4 pieces of straw about 4cm long, corrugated paper, thick card, 4 cotton reels, 40cm dowel, soft wire, two 50cm lengths of elastic bands, a set of running wheels (see page 8) and a set of driving wheels (see page 14), with a crank, made from cheese spread boxes.

The power to drive the wagon is provided by two 50cm lengths of elastic bands.

1 Cut a rectangular hole in the top and bottom of box 1. Cut a rectangular hole in one end. This end is the front.

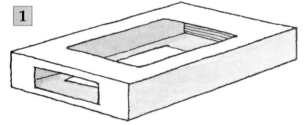

2 Make cuts as shown in the top and bottom of box 2 and fold up the flaps along the dotted lines.

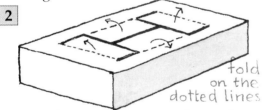

fold on the dotted lines

3 Glue the two boxes together using the flaps on the bottom of box 2 to strengthen the join.

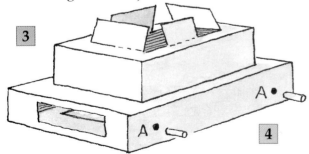

4 Make holes in both sides of box 1 at A and glue in four short pieces of straw as **bearings** for the wheel **axles**.

5 Make holes in both sides of both boxes at B wide enough for the wooden dowel.

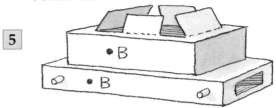

6 Thread the wire **axle** for the running wheels through the straw **bearings** at the back of box 1 and attach the wheels.

7 Bend the wire on the driving wheel **axle** to make a small **crank**. Thread the **axle** through the straw **bearings** from the inside and attach the wheels. Leave enough wire at one end to make a handle.

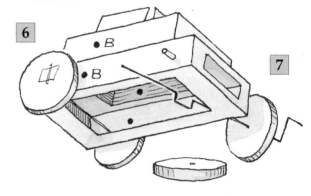

8 Cut two lengths of dowel about 3cm wider than the width of the model. Thread each piece of dowel through a set of holes at B, fitting two **pulleys** on to each dowel as you go.

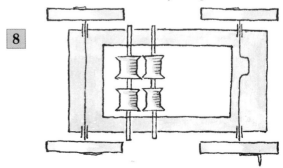

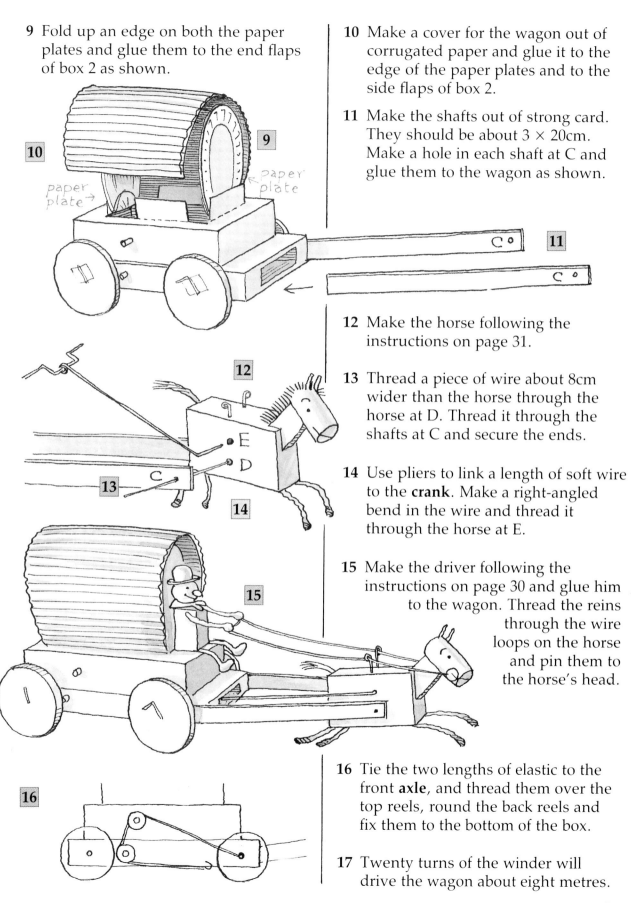

9 Fold up an edge on both the paper plates and glue them to the end flaps of box 2 as shown.

10 Make a cover for the wagon out of corrugated paper and glue it to the edge of the paper plates and to the side flaps of box 2.

11 Make the shafts out of strong card. They should be about 3 × 20cm. Make a hole in each shaft at C and glue them to the wagon as shown.

12 Make the horse following the instructions on page 31.

13 Thread a piece of wire about 8cm wider than the horse through the horse at D. Thread it through the shafts at C and secure the ends.

14 Use pliers to link a length of soft wire to the **crank**. Make a right-angled bend in the wire and thread it through the horse at E.

15 Make the driver following the instructions on page 30 and glue him to the wagon. Thread the reins through the wire loops on the horse and pin them to the horse's head.

16 Tie the two lengths of elastic to the front **axle**, and thread them over the top reels, round the back reels and fix them to the bottom of the box.

17 Twenty turns of the winder will drive the wagon about eight metres.

27

Animated toys

Both the tricycle (page 22) and the wagon (page 26) use a **crank** to make parts of the models come to life. Here are some other ideas for models which use **cranks** to give the appearance of motion.

A pushalong bird

You will need: 2 boxes (1 large box about 20 × 9 × 5cm, 1 small box about 9 × 7 × 3cm), a toilet roll, cardboard and paper for the wings, a set of driving wheels (see page 14), made from jam jar lids with a small crank (see page 26), a straw, 30cm of strong wire and some thin wire.

1 Cut a 4cm square hole in the middle of the top and bottom of the large box.

2 Make the driving wheels with a small **crank** in the middle and a short straw **bearing** on either side of the **crank**. The driving wheel **axle** should be about 2cm wider than the large box.

3 Cut a piece of strong wire about 15cm long and wind one end around the **crank**. Make a loop at the other end.

4 Thread the wire through the holes in the box. Tape the straw bearings to the base of the box so that the **crank** can turn in the hole.

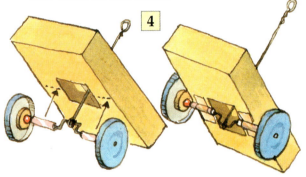

5 Attach two 10cm lengths of thin wire to the loop at the top.

6 Make holes with an awl in both sides of the small box at A. Open out the flaps at one end.

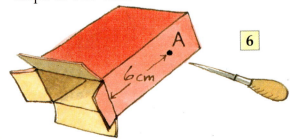

7 Feed one of the lengths of wire attached to the loop through one of the holes at A in the small box. Do the same with the other wire.

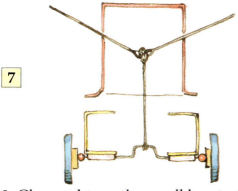

8 Glue and tape the small box to the big box.

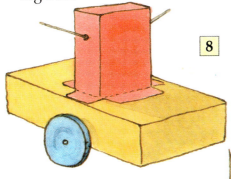

9 Make cuts in the top and bottom of the toilet roll as shown.

10 Glue the flaps at the top together to make a head-shape and fan out the flaps at the bottom. Glue the head to the small box and add a paper beak.

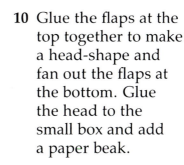
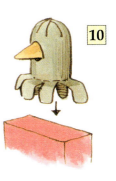

11 Make the wings out of cardboard and tape them to the wires. Add paper feathers, feet and a tail.

12 Attach a 30cm length of wire to the back of the box so that you can push the bird along. As the wheels turn, the **crank** should make the wings flap.

See if you can make the horse gallop, Strong Man Sam lift the weights and the goat trot.

The drivers . . .

The drivers for your models can be made from corks, boxes, pipe-cleaners and bottle tops and dressed with scraps of cloth. Here are some ideas to help you.

Wire figures

1 Twist wire or pipe-cleaners on to a button to make the head and body shape.

2 Make the head and hair and simple clothes out of scraps of cloth.

Racing driver (page 9)

1 Cut a sweet tube in half, **diagonally**.

2 Make holes at A and B and insert pipe-cleaners for the arms and legs.

3 Paint a face on a cork and glue it into the top of the tube.

4 Make a crash helmet out of a wire cap from a fizzy wine bottle, and make a visor from a strip of plastic.

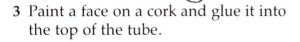

Tractor driver (page 19)

1 Cut a sweet tube in two, **diagonally**.

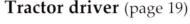

2 Turn the pieces around until they join together almost at a right angle. Tape them together. Repeat this with three more sweet tubes.

3 Glue them to a large matchbox to make arms and legs. Cut the ends of the arms to make fingers and add thin matchboxes to the legs to make feet.

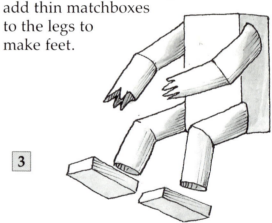

4 Tape two small plastic pots together to make the head and hat. Add a paper nose and paint the eyes and mouth.

Tricyclist (page 23)

1 Make the head from half a toilet roll tube. Make cuts in one end as shown. Fold in the points and tape them together. Add a paper nose and paint the eyes and mouth. Cut a shape from an eggbox for the hat.

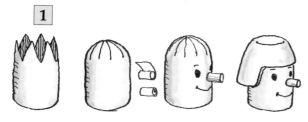

2 Glue the head to a large matchbox. Make holes at A and thread a length of wire through to make the arms.

3 Glue the body on to the tricycle seat and cover her arms and legs with pieces of material.

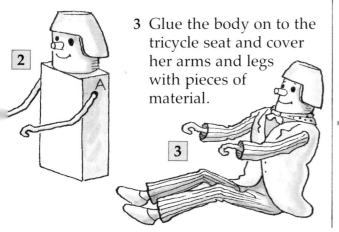

Wagon driver (page 26)

1 Cut a 2cm slice from a cork and glue it to another cork with a circle of paper in between. Paint a face.

2 Make holes in either side of a film box at A and thread a 30cm piece of string through the holes to make the arms and reins.

3 Thread a piece of straw and a bead on to each end of the string. Tie a knot after the bead to stop the arms slipping.

4 Attach pipe-cleaner legs and feet. Glue the head to the body and add a tissue paper scarf.

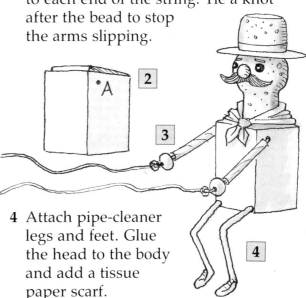

and the horse (page 26)

1 Make a cut in the small matchbox as shown. Glue it to the large matchbox and cork.

2 Use string or wool to make the legs, mane and tail.

3 Make holes on each side of the matchbox at A and B.

4 Make two small holes at C. Push a 10cm length of wire through each hole and make a loop at the top.

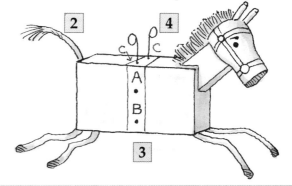

Decorating your models

The models will be easier to decorate if you paint them all over with emulsion paint first. You can also use paint to cover metal jam jar lid wheels. Paint the wheels a dark colour, then add silver or white spokes.

Put on the details with felt pens or paints.

Details on the cars and trucks can be drawn on paper and glued on, or use sticky-backed paper.

Use pieces of sticky paper to put your own name on the trucks.

Toothpaste caps can be glued on as lamps.